For Bill,

Warm Regards from Alaska.

Michael Klennak
7/17/02

YUKON • ALASKA • BRITISH COLUMBIA

Aurora's Winter Waltz

Photography and Essays *by* Michael Klensch

Aurora's Winter Waltz
Yukon - Alaska - British Columbia
Northern Lights Photography by Michael Klensch

ISBN-10: 0-9779070-0-7
ISBN-13: 978-0-9779070-0-7

Created and designed by C. E. Furbish & Michael Klensch
Published by Alpenglow Photo in the United States
Printed in Hong Kong

ALPENGLOW
PHOTO

P.O. Box 1076
Skagway, AK 99840
mike@aglowphoto.com
www.aglowphoto.com

I am sincerely grateful to the many friends and family members
who contributed their time and encouragement with the editing
and reviewing of this book. And especial heartfelt thanks go out
to Elaine. Without her hard work, skills and patience, this book
would not have been possible.
                                                        - Mike

Front Cover: "Yukon Magic"

Back Cover: "A Midwinter Night's Dream"

Right: One thin auroral ray pierces the sky.

Far right: Green lights over the Taiya Inlet
              and the distant Chilkat Mountains.

For Bonnie, who taught me how to see.

"We of the night will know many things
of which you sleepers will never dream."

Bessie Hyde

ABOVE
Multicolored auroral curtain over White Pass, at the Alaska-Canada Border.

"... as the all-cheering sun
Should in the furthest east begin to draw
The shady curtains from Aurora's bed..."

William Shakespeare
Romeo and Juliet

In Roman mythology, Aurora is the beautiful goddess of dawn. She flies across the sky and opens the gates of heaven, announcing the arrival of her brother Sol, the sun god, who drives his chariot across the sky each morning.

During winter months at far northern latitudes, Sol tends to rise lazily and late, and then only for an ephemeral appearance. Aurora enthusiastically compensates for her coy brother's procrastination by languidly waltzing across northern night skies, to the serenade of howling wolves and applause of twinkling stars. Among Aurora's extended family are her sister, Luna, the moon goddess, and her sons the four winds: north, south, east and west.

Galileo first used the term "aurora borealis" in 1619 to describe a glowing light he witnessed one evening on the distant northern horizon. This Latin phrase means northern (borealis) dawn (aurora). The aurora is also commonly known as the "northern lights".

ABOVE
Double auroral arcs stretch across Tutshi (pronounced "too-shy") Lake in northern British Columbia, creating an early autumn dreamscape.

ABOVE
Red over green rayed bands shine above Mount Harding, Skagway, Alaska.

ABOVE
A photon lasso about to ensnare Racine Mountain, Yukon Territory.

RIGHT
A gentle shower of light appears to rain down upon a fortunate tree.

Northern lights legends have been passed down through many generations of storytellers. One Native Alaskan tale describes how people who depart this life will move on to various places in the hereafter depending on their individual qualities such as courage and generosity. The highest level of heaven is within the aurora where beauty abounds and the living is easy.

Science analytically explains how aurorae occur when energy from the sun enters and excites gases within Earth's atmosphere. However, people fortunate enough to witness an auroral display will appreciate the Native mythology and be inspired to work on their virtues of benevolence and charity.

L E F T
*Unusually large and well
defined auroral rays are
thrown down like celestial
spears on Face Mountain
in Skagway, Alaska.*

RIGHT

The Valkyries of Norse mythology were beautiful young women riding winged horses. Their shimmering armor was thought to create the aurora.

Above this foggy lake in the southern Yukon Territory, the Valkyries appear to ride again... whisking brave warriors off to Valhalla.

LEFT
Celestial Song

RIGHT
An ethereal turquoise wisp appears to rise from Face Mountain in Skagway, Alaska.

Cause and Effect

To understand what you are looking at, this double exposure image requires some explanation.

People frequently ask me... "What causes the aurora?". So I had the idea of creating a composition that would depict both an aurora and its "source" in one photograph.

The primary catalyst for auroral activity is the sun... charged particles are thrown off into space and make up an energy stream called the "solar wind". Some of this wind intercepts Earth, and although our planet's magnetic field deflects most of the energy, some gets funneled into the upper atmosphere where the field is weakest, near the north and south poles. At very high altitudes, the charged solar particles interact with atmospheric gases and create the glow of an aurora. Auroral displays in the northern hemisphere are called "aurora borealis", while those in the southern hemisphere are called "aurora australis".

Most energy contained within the solar wind is released during massive solar flares and coronal mass ejections (CMEs). These huge solar eruptions emanate from relatively cool, and therefore dark, regions where magnetic force-fields poke through the sun's surface. These dark areas are called "sunspots", which can be many times the diameter of the Earth in size. It takes an average of two days for the stream of plasma released in a solar explosion to reach the Earth.

The large red object in the upper right of this image is the sun, and you will notice a few sunspot groups. The larger sunspot group to the left comprises an area greater than five Earth diameters.

I photographed the sun through a telescope with a special solar filter (NEVER look directly at the sun without a special solar filter!). As it happened, there was a CME that day. Two nights later when the energy from the CME reached Earth, I exposed the same frame of film with a wide-angle lens to capture the aurora.

Thus, this double exposure photograph displays the sunspots (cause) along with the auroral display (effect) that resulted from that solar activity.

BELOW
An unusual magenta hue compliments white-green rays.

ABOVE
A red bulls-eye is framed between green and cyan on a bright moonlit evening.

The most common aurora colors are shades of green. However, displays of white, yellow, blue, purple and red can also be seen.

Incoming solar particles collide with and excite atmospheric gases in ways that produce specific colors. Colors will vary depending upon the type and density of these gases. The colors our eyes perceive are also largely determined by our sensitivity to specific wavelengths. Our eyes are more sensitive to green than they are to red. This predisposition in part leads to seeing green displays more readily than other colors. Red is usually only perceived during very strong solar storms. Other atmospheric influences such as bright moonlight or diffuse clouds can also alter auroral hues.

RIGHT
Well defined multicolored rayed bands above the Sawtooth Mountains in Skagway, Alaska.

LEFT
A delicate cyan ribbon reaches out to play with the constellation Orion.

RIGHT
The subtle beauty of a faint white aurora in a star-splashed night sky is captured in black and white.

LEFT
A brilliant green rayed auroral band emulates the contours of Parson's Peak and reflects upon Nahku Bay in Skagway, Alaska.

RIGHT
A multicolored fan unfolds across the subarctic night sky above northern British Columbia.

ABOVE
A green auroral blanket covers Skagway, Alaska in this photograph taken from the end of the railroad dock, on the southeast side of town. Looking north, AB Mountain separates the Taiya Valley (left) from the Skagway Valley (right).

I live in Skagway, a small community in southeast Alaska. The town is located at the end of Lynn Canal, a deep saltwater fjord. While the Skagway waterfront remains lit during winter, the cruise ship docks will not see activity again until spring. Winter is a time for residents to reflect on the beauty of living in the North Country. The hustle and bustle of summer tourist season is replaced with short, crisp, quiet days and long nights illuminated by frequent aurorae.

RIGHT

A bright moon and Venus peek above the mountain tops and rise into a star-dusted, aurora-tinted night sky. The Skagway railroad dock is seen to the left.

L E F T
The road north leads to the Big Dipper poised between auroral arcs.

Klondike Highway links Skagway with Whitehorse, the capital of the Yukon Territory. This 99-mile highway connects to the Alaska Highway - and through it to the rest of the continental road system.

RIGHT

Star trails pirouette over Moore Creek Bridge, Skagway, Alaska, while a soft green aurora illuminates the horizon.

The "trails" are rings of light that stars left behind as they traveled across the sky during this two hour exposure. The point of light around which the other stars appear to travel is the North Star – Polaris. Because Polaris is almost directly above the Earth's north celestial pole, it moves least, while stars farther away from this point move more… creating the pinwheel effect over time.

A B O V E
A vibrant beam of aurora ignites the Yukon sky and surrounding landscape with an icy-red fire.

A Midwinter Night's Dream

I was busily organizing my camera bag. I knew protons and electrons would bombard the planet that evening from a massive solar storm that occurred two days earlier. When solar winds hit the Earth's magnetic field, the night sky would come alive with dancing ribbons, curtains, bands and arcs of auroral color. I was preparing for a blissfully sleepless night out watching the subarctic sky.

It was early, maybe 6:00 p.m. when I first poked my head out into the cold night air. Looking up, I was both disappointed and astounded with what I saw. The sky over my town, Skagway Alaska, was mostly covered in clouds, but they glowed red from the intensely bright aurora that burned above them.

I threw on my parka, insulated pants and bunny boots, slung the tripod over my shoulder and jumped in the truck, camera gear spilling from my arms.

I drove north in the hopes I would find clear skies on the drier Canada side of the Coastal Mountain Range just 15 miles away. However, it was after driving 40 miles that I finally emerged under stars.

I pulled off of the road next to a large glacially carved lake that had yet to freeze for the winter. Leaving the truck, I stepped into a surreal dream where the surrounding snow covered landscape glowed red from the icy fire that blazed above. Surging red waves of light, such as I had never seen, engulfed me. Red aurorae are rare, usually transient and have little structure, but after two hours next to that lake the display never dimmed or changed color. When clouds from the south finally cloaked the sky, I happily resigned to drive back to town, more than

enthralled with one of the most beautiful and unusual auroral displays I had ever seen.

Coasting down the south side of the mountain pass, I was amazed to see that skies above Skagway were now clear. I arrived home around midnight and decided to hike out to a

ABOVE

The V-shaped star cluster, Hyades, points toward a bright red curtain of aurora illuminating sky, mountain top and water.

rocky granite finger of land that juts out into the deep saltwater fjord that meets the town to the south. Walking through the forest, there was no need to use my headlamp as the trail was illuminated by the aurora that pulsated overhead and the nearly full moon, with its dance partner for that evening, Jupiter, that had just risen above the steep mountains to the east.

There was no wind that night as I sat on a huge boulder at the very tip of the peninsula. Calm waters reflected the sky and shimmered red. It was perfectly still... where did the sky begin? Was there truly water at my feet, or was I floating upon a sea of celestial wonderment?

Suddenly, but softly, the stillness was broken by a familiar sound... a deep and long exhalation of whale breath. I wasn't alone. Red, aurora-reflected ripples traveled away from the humpback as she slid back into her liquid realm, finally defining the still waters. A few moments later, another breath, but this one

was different... shorter and higher pitched... and then some singing. A calf was joining the mother whale for a midnight swim. Were they curious to know why their normally inky black surrounding shone red? Were they also taking a moment to revel in the magic of that night?

Then came more familiar sounds from other masters of the water world. A number of seal heads emerged to breathe the cold night air and to bark at each other. Or were they barking at me for arrogantly occupying their favorite haul-out rock? Whatever their reasons, we were all aware of each other's presence and decided to collectively share in this fantasy. Then I remembered the ancient Native legend of Nunivak Island, Alaska where it was believed the aurora is a game of celestial football played by spirit walruses. Were their kin now simply showing up to enjoy the game?

Skies remained alive with dancing light and my marine companions were still swimming through glowing waters when I decided to head for home at 4:00 a.m. My eyes were heavy and my senses overwhelmed. I knew it was time for my conscious mind to rest and my unconscious mind to dream. But could there ever be an unconscious dream as sweet?

"And the skies of night
    were alive with light,
    with a throbbing,
    thrilling flame;

Amber and rose and violet,
    opal and gold it came.

It swept the sky like a
    giant scythe,
    it quivered back to
    a wedge;

Argently bright,
    it cleft the night
    with a wavy golden edge."

Robert W. Service
"The Ballad of the
Northern Lights"

LEFT
Fantasia Borealis

ABOVE
Birkeland's Quiescence

A silvery full moon is joined by a fiery red curtain of aurora tinged with green. This photo is a tribute to Norwegian scientist Kristian Birkeland. While his findings were largely ignored for decades, his lab and field work in the late 1800s and early 1900s first revealed the true workings of the aurora.

ABOVE
Nahku Bay Nocturne

RIGHT
An early autumn aurora shimmers over snow-free mountains and the unfrozen Tutshi Lake, northern British Columbia.

ABOVE
This unwavering auroral band, tinted blue by a full moon, casts its hue to the surrounding snow-covered landscape.

RIGHT
A fast moving white-green aurora appears to rip open the Alaskan sky.

ABOVE
A brush-stroke of twisted auroral ribbons above Mount Conrad in the Yukon Territory.

A B O V E
Aurora, stars, the moon and Venus - all join in a celestial ballet over Tutshi Lake, northern British Columbia.

LEFT
Looking directly overhead into an auroral corona, light emanates from one point and spreads in all directions.

ABOVE
Red, green and cyan rays dance above the moonlit Sawtooth Mountains near Skagway, Alaska.

LEFT AND ABOVE
*Auroral bands and Comet
Hale-Bopp play above Rock Creek
in Denali National Park, Alaska.*

ABOVE
Comet Hale-Bopp skirts between twin auroral arcs near the Savage River,
Denali National Park, Alaska.

LEFT
Like an unravelling valentine, this aurora drops from the heavens near White Pass, Skagway, Alaska.

RIGHT
Twisted and rayed auroral arcs whip across a star-studded sky.

LEFT
A soft green crescent tinged with purple glows above the Alaskan landscape.

ABOVE
A Midwinter Night's Dream

ABOVE
*The planet Mars casts a blazing red
streak across Tutshi Lake in northern
British Columbia.*

RIGHT
*Three stars form a tiara over the moon,
while Venus perches at the tip of Witch
Mountain in Skagway, Alaska.*

"Nothing more wonderfully beautiful can exist than the Arctic night. It is a dreamland, painted in the imagination's most delicate tints; it is color etherealized. ... it is all faint, dreamy color music, a far-away, long-drawn-out melody on muted strings."

Fridtjof Nansen
Farthest North

Even when Aurora is reluctant to make her appearance, high northern latitude night skies are no less spectacular. Mother Nature uses the dark and transparent arctic air as the perfect canvas upon which she paints her cosmologic masterpieces.

ABOVE
Sometimes the setting sun can reflect off of high clouds to create a "false aurora". Here Comet Hale-Bopp peeks through pastel magenta clouds for a twilight encounter above Denali National Park, Alaska.

47

Perseus hurtles over the rising moon with Comet Hale-Bopp in his hip pocket.

Perseus is the mythical Greek hero who rescued the Egyptian princess, Andromeda. He runs to the left with his head thrown back, his pointed cap formed by the triangle of three stars in the top right corner.

Above and to the right of the moon are the Pleiades. This tiny dipper-shaped star cluster is also called "the seven sisters". While most people can only make out six stars with their naked eyes, it blossoms into dozens of the most stunning celestial jewels when viewed with simple binoculars.

The "Great Hunter" of Greek mythology, Orion, was placed into the heavens after his death. In this image, the great hunter steps lightly over mountain tops, wielding his club and shield as he scans the "Great Land" of Alaska for his next quarry.

Across the deep saltwater fjord that defines Skagway's southern border, one sees a perfect and complete portrait of the great hunter. The three stars comprising Orion's belt, along with the stars in his sword, are the most recognizable grouping in the constellation. However, the bright stars Bellatrix (left shoulder), Rigel (left foot) and red Betelgeuse (right shoulder) also blaze distinctly in the cold night sky.

L E F T
The crystal clear and dark skies of far northern latitudes are perfect for gazing into the arms of our 150,000 light-year wide celestial neighborhood, the Milky Way Galaxy.

ABOVE

A delicate pastel aurora and moon join a rare planetary alignment to inspire an otherworldly scene. The brightest star-like object close to the horizon and reflected in the lake is the planet Venus, the slightly dimmer point above it is the planet Jupiter and the point just to the left of the moon is the planet Saturn.

"I heard the trailing
        garments of the Night
Sweep through her
        marble halls!

I saw her sable skirts
        all fringed with light
From the celestial walls!

I felt her presence, by its
        spell of might,
Stoop o'er me from above;

The calm, majestic
        presence of the Night,
As of the one I love."

Henry Wadsworth Longfellow
                Hymn to the Night

LEFT
A double curtain falls over an early autumn hillside.

ABOVE
Strong auroral arcs flare above Lime Mountain and Tagish Lake, Yukon Territory.

ABOVE
A late summer sky is just dark enough to reveal the first aurora of the new season in northern British Columbia.

RIGHT
Twisting auroral rays seem as icy cold as the frozen winter lake over which they dance in the southern Yukon Territory.

LEFT
Wraiths of ghostly light waver in the autumn night.

ABOVE
A quick twist of green aurora twirls in Yukon skies and then vanishes into the moonlight.

ABOVE
A translucent rainbow of auroral rays plays with the clouds over Nahku Bay, Skagway, Alaska.

RIGHT
The embodiment of grace, an elegant aurora curves into a wooded hillside in northern British Columbia.

LEFT
The sky is ablaze with incandescent flames of red and yellow in northern British Columbia.

ABOVE
A celestial eye peers down upon planet Earth.

ABOVE
The season's first snow blankets the shore and mountains, while a soft green aurora and an evening mist rise over unfrozen Tutshi Lake, northern British Columbia.

About the Photographer

As a Skagway, Alaska resident and freelance landscape photographer, I look to the natural beauty that surrounds me everyday for limitless photographic inspiration and adventure. Educated and trained in environmental sciences, I have spent much of my career working for a number of National Parks across the country. Exposure to the beauty of the natural world has created a personal passion for the preservation and stewardship of nature, which I express through photography.

I have always been, and continue to be awe-struck by the incredible beauty and variety in wild landscapes. However, true wilderness is just as threatened with extinction as the many species of flora and fauna that seek sanctuary within its protective borders. To see the beauty and magic of the natural world with one's own eyes is to comprehend how truly fortunate we are to share this extraordinarily beautiful planet. By recording some of this magic with my camera, I hope to inspire others to see wilderness with wonder, respect and humility. For by seeing in this manner, we might then be willing to preserve these special places for the future generations from whom they are borrowed.

The images in this book are 35mm format film photographs. Except for the double exposure

on page 15, there are no "tricks" to my photography. In fact, it is rather low-tech compared to the techniques and equipment generally used by today's professionals. The aurora images are not filtered or altered.

The grandeur of snow-capped mountains, deep blue icy fjords, crystal clear alpine lakes, and star-filled, auroral painted night skies continue to inspire and stir emotions that are hard to put into words. It is my sincere wish that these photographs communicate where words fail.

Michael Klensch